THE TINY PERFECT
DINOSAUR
BOOK TWO

Presenting Tyrannosaurus Rex

ussell

S   ISHING

Toronto

Contents

The King of Dinosaurs 3

Amazing Dinosaurs 4

This Is Tyrannosaurus Rex 7

Discovery of Tyrannosaurus 8

How Did Tyrannosaurus Become a Fossil? 10

The Time of the Dinosaurs 12

Family Tree 14

The World of Tyrannosaurus 16

Tyrannosaurus's Neighbors 18

Inside Tyrannosaurus's Head...........................22

Hand and Foot 24

Predator or Scavenger? 26

Moving Fast 28

Why Dinosaurs Became Extinct 30

Farewell to Tyrannosaurus 32

Farewell to Tyrannosaurus

Tyrannosaurus was the biggest predator ever to live on land, and it had the biggest teeth of any dinosaur. With its huge head, sharp eyes, strange front legs, and powerful back legs, it terrorized all western North America during the last part of the age of the dinosaurs.

Even though *Tyrannosaurus* is gone forever, it will always be a favorite of scientists and people who like dino- saurs. Together we will keep it alive in our imaginations.

The King of Dinosaurs

Of all the scary animals that ever lived, *Tyrannosaurus* (tye-RAN-o-SORE-us) was the scariest. It was very large and had long, sharp teeth that it used to eat other animals. Its name means tyrant lizard (a tyrant is a nasty sort of king). The second part of its name is *rex*, which also means king.

Amazing Dinosaurs

A long time ago, dinosaurs roamed the earth. But now they are all gone. The last dinosaur died long before any of us were born.

Dinosaurs were reptiles, like lizards and snakes. Although some were as small as a pigeon, some, like *Tyrannosaurus*, were the size of a bus. All of them were bare-skinned. Most of them laid eggs. And they all held their bodies high off the ground.

Unlike dragons, which are imaginary, dinosaurs really lived on earth. But like dragons, some were quite terrifying. (The name dinosaur means terrible lizard.)

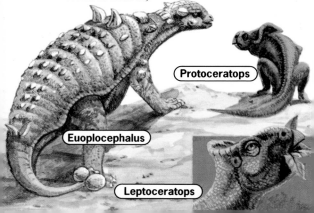

Protoceratops

Euoplocephalus

Leptoceratops

Compsognathus

Spinosaurus

Plateosaurus

5

This Is Tyrannosaurus Rex

The biggest, oldest, meanest *Tyrannosaurus* was about forty-five feet (fourteen meters) long—longer than the longest snakes, the biggest crocodiles, and the largest killer sharks around today. A really big *Tyrannosaurus* would have weighed about five tons (five tonnes), about the same as a bull elephant.

Tyrannosaurus was a predator, which means it ate other animals. Although a few bigger predators have lived in the water, *Tyrannosaurus* was the largest to live on land.

Discovery of Tyrannosaurus

Fossils are made when the bones, teeth, eggs, or footprints of an animal are turned to rock. The first *Tyrannosaurus* fossils were discovered in 1902. A man named Barnum Brown found them in a place called Hell Creek Valley in Montana. When he saw how big *Tyrannosaurus* was and how huge its teeth were, he knew he had made a wonderful discovery. It took him two years to dig the fossils out of the ground, even though he used dynamite for part of the job.

Since then, scientists have found about ten skeletons of *Tyrannosaurus*. Some of them have been broken or incomplete. Paleontologists (PAY-le-on-TAW-lo-jists), people who study fossils, think there are more skeletons waiting to be discovered.

By studying fossils, paleontologists try to guess what the dinosaurs looked like, what they ate, and how they moved around.

Put together the bones that came with this book. (See the back of the poster for exact instructions.) You will have a skeleton of *Tyrannosaurus* like the one found by Barnum Brown.

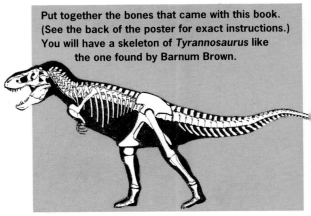

How Did Tyrannosaurus Become a Fossil?

The fossils of *Tyrannosaurus* have been discovered in sandstone. Sandstone is a type of rock that was once sand, particularly the sand that lies at the bottom of a river.

Imagine an old *Tyrannosaurus* with lots of broken bones. He goes to the river for his last drink of water, then lays his head on the ground and dies. Small dinosaurs find the body

A dinosaur dies

It is buried in a river

and eat the big dinosaur's flesh.

A few days later a big rainstorm floods the river, and *Tyrannosaurus*'s body is washed to the bottom of the river, where it is soon buried in the sand. All the flesh rots away until only the bones remain. Over many years the bones turn to fossils, and the sand becomes sandstone.

The bones turn to fossils

The skeleton is discovered

The Time of the Dinosaurs

How long ago did dinosaurs live? They lived so long ago that there were no people at all. Imagine you are watching a speeded-up movie that shows the entire life of the world in one hour. The first twenty-five minutes are boring—just a lot of bad weather. For the next thirty minutes, all you see are ocean creatures, like jellyfish.

With only five minutes to go, you might think nothing much was going to happen.

Life in the ocean

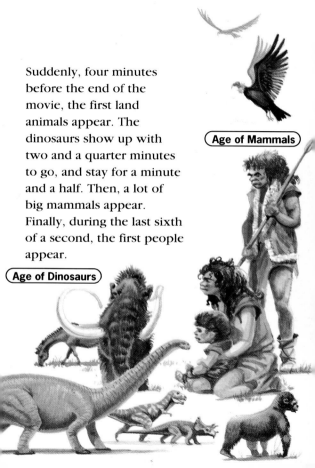

Suddenly, four minutes before the end of the movie, the first land animals appear. The dinosaurs show up with two and a quarter minutes to go, and stay for a minute and a half. Then, a lot of big mammals appear. Finally, during the last sixth of a second, the first people appear.

Age of Mammals

Age of Dinosaurs

Family Tree

Paleontologists classify dinosaurs in many different groups. Here are some of the famous dinosaurs and the groups they belong in.

flying reptiles — — — — — — — — thecodonts

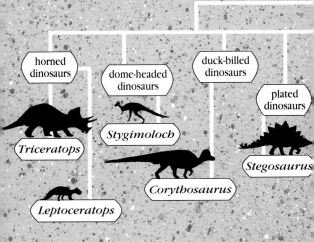

horned dinosaurs

dome-headed dinosaurs

duck-billed dinosaurs

plated dinosaurs

Triceratops

Stygimoloch

Corythosaurus

Stegosaurus

Leptoceratops

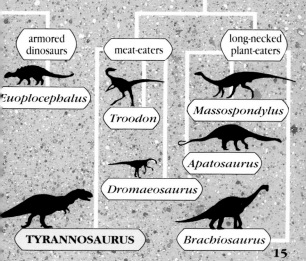

crocodiles and alligators

DINOSAURS

armored dinosaurs

meat-eaters

long-necked plant-eaters

Euoplocephalus

Troodon

Massospondylus

Apatosaurus

Dromaeosaurus

TYRANNOSAURUS

Brachiosaurus

15

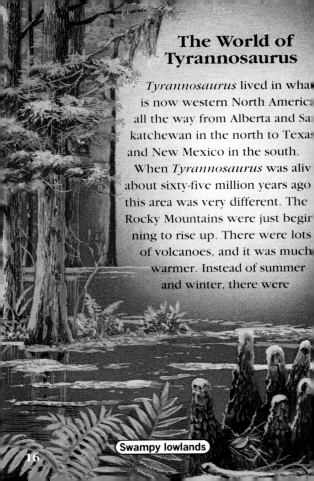

The World of Tyrannosaurus

Tyrannosaurus lived in what is now western North America, all the way from Alberta and Saskatchewan in the north to Texas and New Mexico in the south. When *Tyrannosaurus* was alive, about sixty-five million years ago, this area was very different. The Rocky Mountains were just beginning to rise up. There were lots of volcanoes, and it was much warmer. Instead of summer and winter, there were

Swampy lowlands

Solid green shows the world 65 million years ago. The line shows the map today.

rainy seasons and dry seasons. There were foothills with shrubs and bushes, and swamps with lots of plants and big trees. The uplands in the north were quite cool, but in the south it was hot, especially in the dry season. Unlike some dinosaurs, *Tyrannosaurus* did not have a favorite part of North America. It hunted its prey in all these areas.

Dry uplands

Tyrannosaurus's Neighbors

Tyrannosaurus lived with turtles, crocodiles, small mammals, birds, flying reptiles, snakes, lizards, and insects. After all, dinosaurs were not the only kinds of animals around in those days. One crocodile, *Deinosuchus* (DYE-no-SOO-kuss), was fifty feet (fifteen meters) long, and even *Tyrannosaurus* kept out of its way.

Overhead, *Tyrannosaurus* saw the biggest flying animal of all time, *Quetzalcoatlus* (KET-zal-co-OT-al-us). There were other dinosaurs as well. *Nanotyrannus* (NAN-o-ty-RAN-us) was a meat-eater that looked a lot like *Tyrannosaurus*, but it was smaller, only fifteen feet (five meters) long.

Deinosuchus

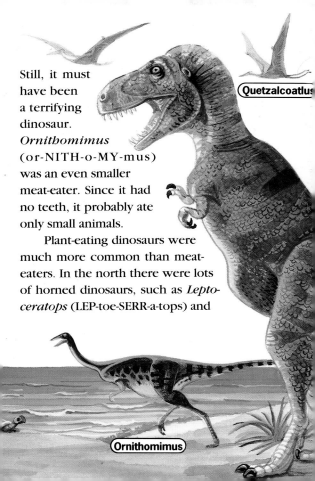

Still, it must have been a terrifying dinosaur. *Ornithomimus* (or-NITH-o-MY-mus) was an even smaller meat-eater. Since it had no teeth, it probably ate only small animals.

Plant-eating dinosaurs were much more common than meat-eaters. In the north there were lots of horned dinosaurs, such as *Leptoceratops* (LEP-toe-SERR-a-tops) and

Quetzalcoatlus

Ornithomimus

Edmontosaurus

Triceratops (try-SERR-a-tops), as well as the duck-billed dinosaur *Edmontosaurus* (ed-MONT-o-SORE-us). In the south, the biggest horned dinosaur was *Torosaurus* (TORE-o-SORE-us), but the long-necked dinosaur *Alamosaurus* (AL-a-mo-SORE-us) was even bigger.

Alamosaurus

Inside Tyrannosaurus's Head

Have a close look at the skull of *Tyrannosaurus*. At the tip of its snout, it had two big nostrils. Scientists think it had a good sense of smell.

Its eyes were small, but it could see well. Unlike those of most other dinosaurs, *Tyrannosaurus*'s eyes faced forward, not out to the sides. This arrangement let it see its prey without turning its head to the side.

Above *Tyrannosaurus*'s eyes, it had two small horns. They weren't very sturdy so no one knows what they were used for.

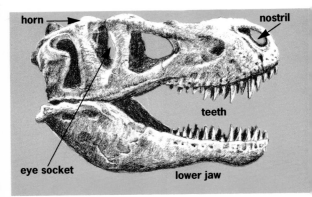

horn → ← nostril

teeth

eye socket

lower jaw

The skull had lots of big holes in it. Some were filled with air to make the head lighter. Others were spaces for muscles to go through. The muscles for the jaws were huge, giving *Tyrannosaurus* great big cheeks.

Tyrannosaurus had the biggest teeth of any dinosaur. It had fifty of them, and the longest were six inches (fifteen centimeters), with cutting edges and sharp tips.

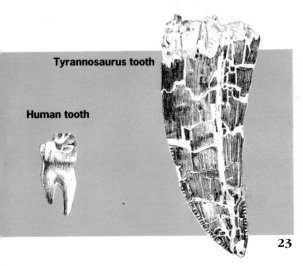

Tyrannosaurus tooth

Human tooth

Hand and Foot

Why were *Tyrannosaurus*'s arms so short that they did not even reach its mouth? That question has puzzled paleontologists since 1902. Maybe *Tyrannosaurus* did not use its arms at all. Or maybe it used them for courting. A *Tyrannosaurus* could tickle the back of another one, or give it a little hug.

One paleontologist thought that *Tyrannosaurus* used its arms to help it stand when it woke up in the morning. Without arms, it might have just pushed its face along the ground with its back legs. Recently, some scientists have decided that perhaps the little arms were very strong and could lift 400 pounds (180 kilograms). If so, *Tyrannosaurus* might have used its arms to hold its struggling prey.

Predator or Scavenger?

The huge pointed teeth and sharp claws of *Tyrannosaurus* are clues that tell us that it ate meat. Most scientists think that it was a very dangerous predator that would sneak up on other dinosaurs and kill them by biting so hard that they bled to death in minutes.

Tyrannosaurus might even have been able to kill huge horned dinosaurs like *Triceratops*, or giant plant-eaters like *Alamosaurus*. These large dinosaurs would have made a big meal for *Tyrannosaurus*, but they had horns and armor to protect themselves. *Triceratops* had horns and *Alamosaurus* may have had pieces of bone right in its skin for protection. But some dinosaurs had no protection. *Edmontosaurus*,

Triceratops

Alamosaurus

Thescelosaur-us (THESS-sell-o-SORE-us), and *Leptoceratops* had to hide or run away when they saw *Tyrannosaurus* coming their way.

Some scientists, however, think that killing was too dangerous for *Tyrannosaurus*. They think it was a scavenger, which means it ate animals that were already dead.

Moving Fast

In the old days, scientists thought that *Tyrannosaurus* stood up straight like a person and dragged its tail. That would have made it very slow moving. Now scientists think it stood with its body tilted over, like a bird's. By holding its tail off the ground, *Tyrannosaurus* could run fast.

How fast could it run? Perhaps as fast as forty-five miles per hour (seventy-two kilometers per hour). More likely, it was slower than that. After all, it weighed as much as an elephant, and elephants can run only twenty miles per hour (thirty-two kilometers per hour).

Why Dinosaurs Became Extinct

Tyrannosaurus was one of the last dinosaurs to live. Many scientists now believe that at the end of the age of dinosaurs a giant meteorite smashed into the earth. It threw up huge clouds of dust and darkened the sky for years. Many plants died. The weather became colder, and the plant-eating dinosaurs died off. With no other dinosaurs to eat, *Tyrannosaurus* became extinct too.

Maybe the last dinosaur alive was a *Tyrannosaurus* that starved to death looking for another dinosaur to eat. Or maybe all the *Tyrannosaurus* died when the meteorite struck. Will we ever know for sure?